BEFORE YOU BEGIN...

Make sure to download the FREE audio program for this book which comes with your purchase! Just go to

www.slangman.com/audio

then look for your book and enter this code:

E2H2AE376W8T

GOLDILOCKS
and the 3 BEARS

Written by: David Burke
Copy Editor: Nili Hirsch and Tami Kamin-Meyer
Illustrated by: "Migs!" Sandoval
Translator: Ofra Obejas
Proofreader: Kai Cofer

Copyright © 2017 by David Burke

Email: info@heywordy.com
Website: www.heywordy.com

Hey Wordy! and all related characters and elements are © and trademarks of Hey Wordy, LLC.

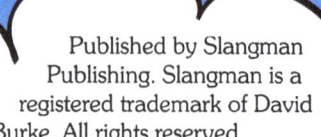

Published by Slangman Publishing. Slangman is a registered trademark of David Burke. All rights reserved. Reproduction or translation of any part of this work beyond that permitted by section 107 or 108 of the 1976 United States Copyright Act without the permission of the copyright owner is unlawful. Requests for permission or further information should be addressed to the Permissions Department, Slangman Publishing. This publication is designed to provide accurate and authoritative information in regard to the subject matter covered. The persons, entities and events in this book are fictitious. Any similarities with actual persons or entities, past and present, are purely coincidental.

ISBN13: 978-1-891888-54-0

Printed in the U.S.A.

Meet the Author
David Burke

Creator and star of the children's TV show, *Hey Wordy!*, David Burke has been single-handedly revolutionizing the foreign language-learning movement worldwide.

In addition to being a performer of boundless energy and enthusiasm, David speaks seven languages. A successful author and entrepreneur, he has built a thriving international publishing company featuring over 100 books he has written for teen/adults & children. His books have won publishing awards and have sold more than one million copies. David's Street Speak™ and Biz Speak™ series of books and audio programs are used around the world by government agencies, leading universities and major corporations.

Since age 4, David has been a classically trained pianist and uses his musical gifts to compose and perform original songs for his TV series, *Hey Wordy!* which introduces children to foreign languages and cultures through music, animation, and magical adventures. He has also composed, orchestrated, and performed all the music in the audio programs for each of these books.

David's engaging and charismatic persona became a fixture on broadcast entertainment channels around the world, such as CNN and the BBC. David and his work have been highlighted in many major publications, including The Los Angeles Times, The Chicago Tribune and The Christian Science Monitor.

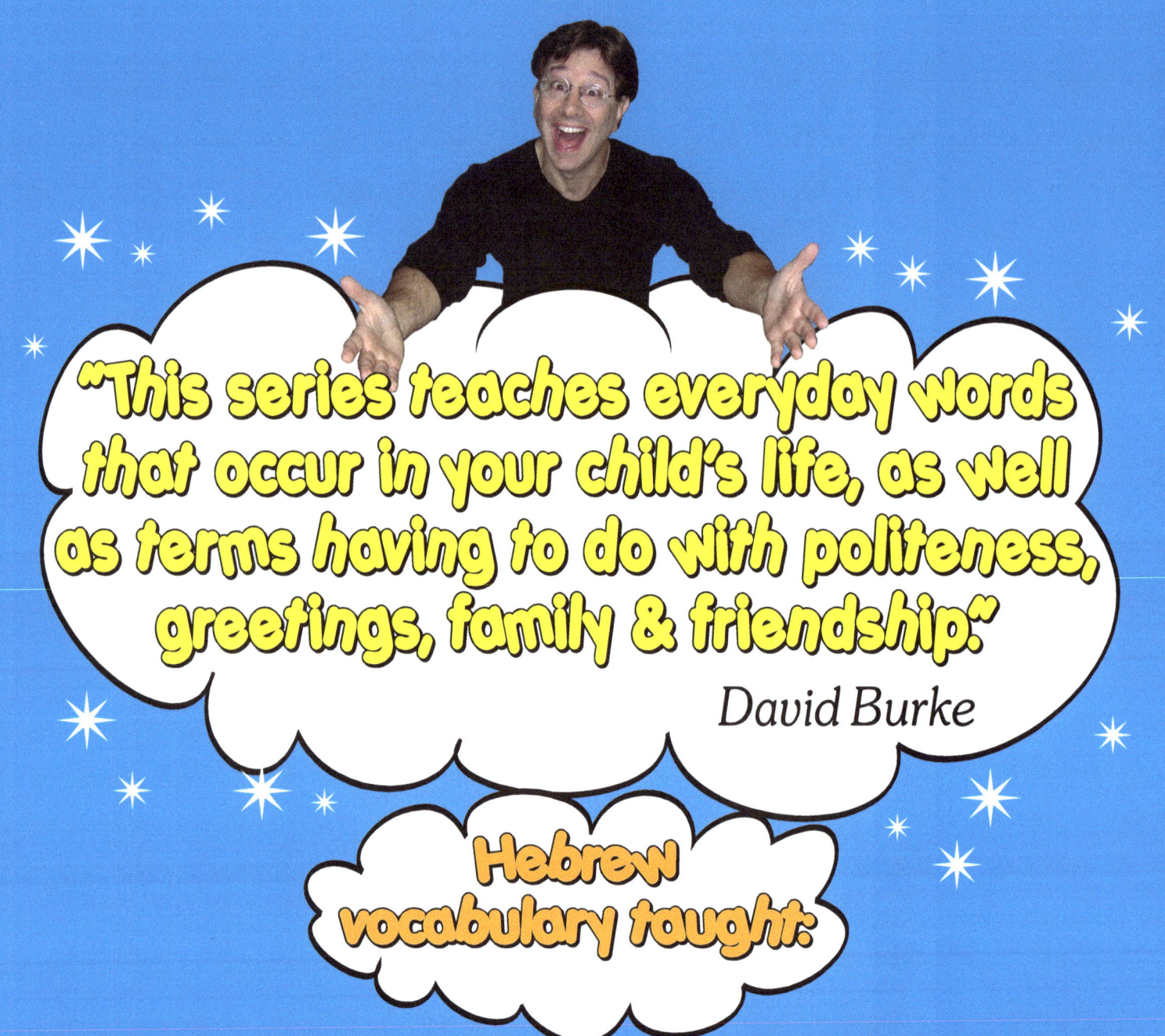

One thing to remember...

The words in *green italics* throughout this fairy tale are words you've already learned in the previous level! Do you still remember what they mean?

from Cindellera (Level 1)

ahavah (אהבה) = love
al lo davar (על לא דבר) = you're welcome
atzuvah (עצובה) = sad
bayit (בית) = house
chatzot (חצות) = midnight
gdola (גדולה) = big
ishah (אישה) = wife
kaf regel (כף רגל) = foot
le'hitra'ot (להיתראות) = goodbye
mesibah (מסיבה) = party

na'al (נעל) = shoe
nasich (נסיך) = prince
ra'ah (רעה) = mean
rega (רגע) = moment
simlah (שמלה) = dress
smechah (שמחה) = happy
todah (תודה) = thank you
yafah (יפה) = pretty
yafeh (יפה) = handsome
yaldah (ילדה) = girl

1

dov
דב

abba
אבא

ima
אמא

Once upon a time, there was a [bear] family. The **dov** family lived in a *bayit* in the forest. There was a [papa] **dov**, a [mama] who was very *yafah*, and their pride and joy,

a child dov who was very little. The **yeled dov**, who was very **katan**, was also very *yafeh* like his **abba**. The **abba dov** had great *ahavah* for the **ima**

→ **yeled** ילד
→ **katan** קטן

and they were indeed proud of their family. One day, the **ima** prepared some soup for lunch, but it was too hot. While it cooled off, the **dov** family went for a [stroll].

tiyul טיול

Meanwhile in a town nearby lived a *yaldah* named Goldilocks who was very *atzuvah* because she was so tired of never having anything fun to do.

She thought for a *rega* and came up with an idea. She decided to take a **tiyul** in the forest. Very soon, she came upon a *bayit* and knocked on the door but no one

delet דלת

was there. So she opened the **delet**, put one *kaf regel* inside the *bayit*, and said "Hello? Is anyone home?" She was very tired after her long **tiyul**

ayefah
עייפה

shulchan שלחן
mitbach מיטבח

and since no one answered, she walked inside the **bayit**. She looked around for a **rega** and was very **smechah** to see a table in the kitchen with food piled high on it!

Goldilocks quickly walked toward the **shulchan** in the **mitbach** and was super extra **smechah** because there on the **shulchan** in the **mitbach** was a bowl – **ke'arah** קערה

echad אחד
shtayim שתים
shalosh שלוש

but not just one, not just two, but three! **Echad**, **shtayim**, **shalosh**! And the smell from each **ke'arah** was wonderful! So, she took a taste from the **ke'arah** that

belonged to the **abba dov**, and said, "This is too hot ！" Then she took a taste from the **ke'arah** that belonged to the **ima** and said, "Oh! This is too cold !" Then she took a taste

cham
חם

kar
קר

from the **ke'arah** of the **yeled dov** and said, "This one isn't too **cham**. It isn't too **kar**. It's just right!" And she ate everything in the **ke'arah**. "*Todah*!" she said to the

empty **ke'arah**. Well, now she was even more **ayefah** than ever after eating so much food. So, she decided to rest. In the living room, she saw an armchair...but not just

kursah
כורסא

echad, not just shtayim, but shalosh! Echad, shtayim, shalosh! So, she sat down in the first kursah of the abba dov and said, "Oh! This kursah is too

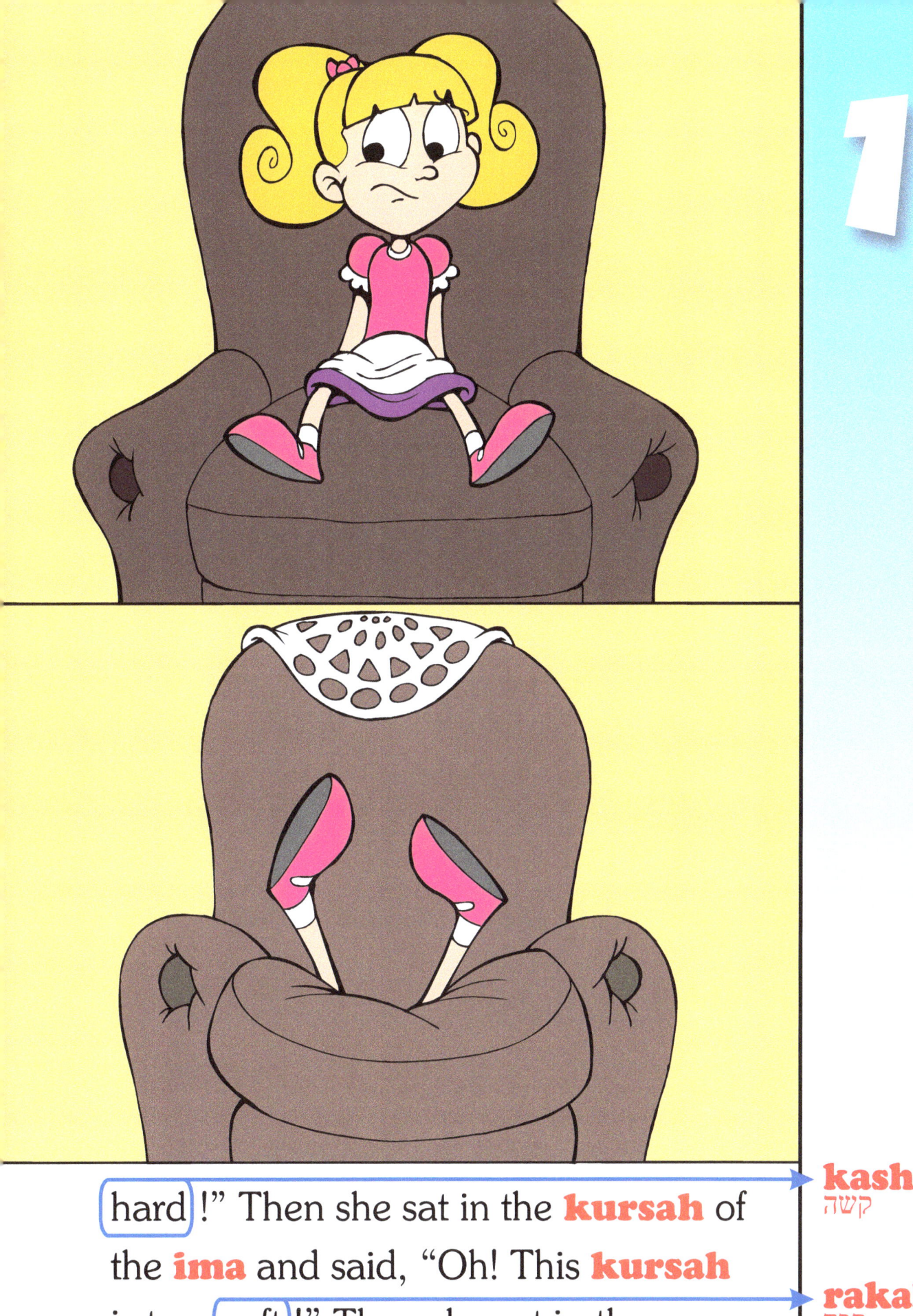

hard!" Then she sat in the **kursah** of the **ima** and said, "Oh! This **kursah** is too soft!" Then she sat in the **kursah** of the **yeled dov** and said,

kashah קשה

rakah רכה

15

"Ah. This one isn't too **kashah**. It isn't too **rakah**. It's just right!" But just as she got comfortable…*Crack!* The **kursah** of the **yeled dov** broke and completely fell apart!

Still **ayefah**, she decided to look for the bedroom to take a little nap. In front of her, she saw a bed, but not just **echad**, not just **shtayim**, but **shalosh**!

mitah
מיטה

Echad, **shtayim**, **shalosh**! So, she tried the **mitah** that belonged to the **abba dov** and said, "This **mitah** is too **kashah**!" Then she tried the **mitah** that belonged to the **ima** and

said, "This **mitah** is too **rakah**!" Then she tried the **mitah** of the **yeled dov** and said, "Ah. This one isn't too **kashah**. It isn't too **rakah**. It's just right!" And she fell

19

asleep. At that **rega**, the **dov** family returned from their **tiyul**. Upon entering the **bayit**, the **abba dov** noticed something strange. "Someone's been eating my soup!" he said.

"And someone's been eating my soup!" said the confused **ima**. "And someone's been eating MY soup and ate it all up!" cried the **yeled dov**.

"Look!" said the **abba dov**, who was getting angrier, "Someone's been sitting in my **kursah**!" Then the **ima** said, "And someone's been sitting in my **kursah**!"

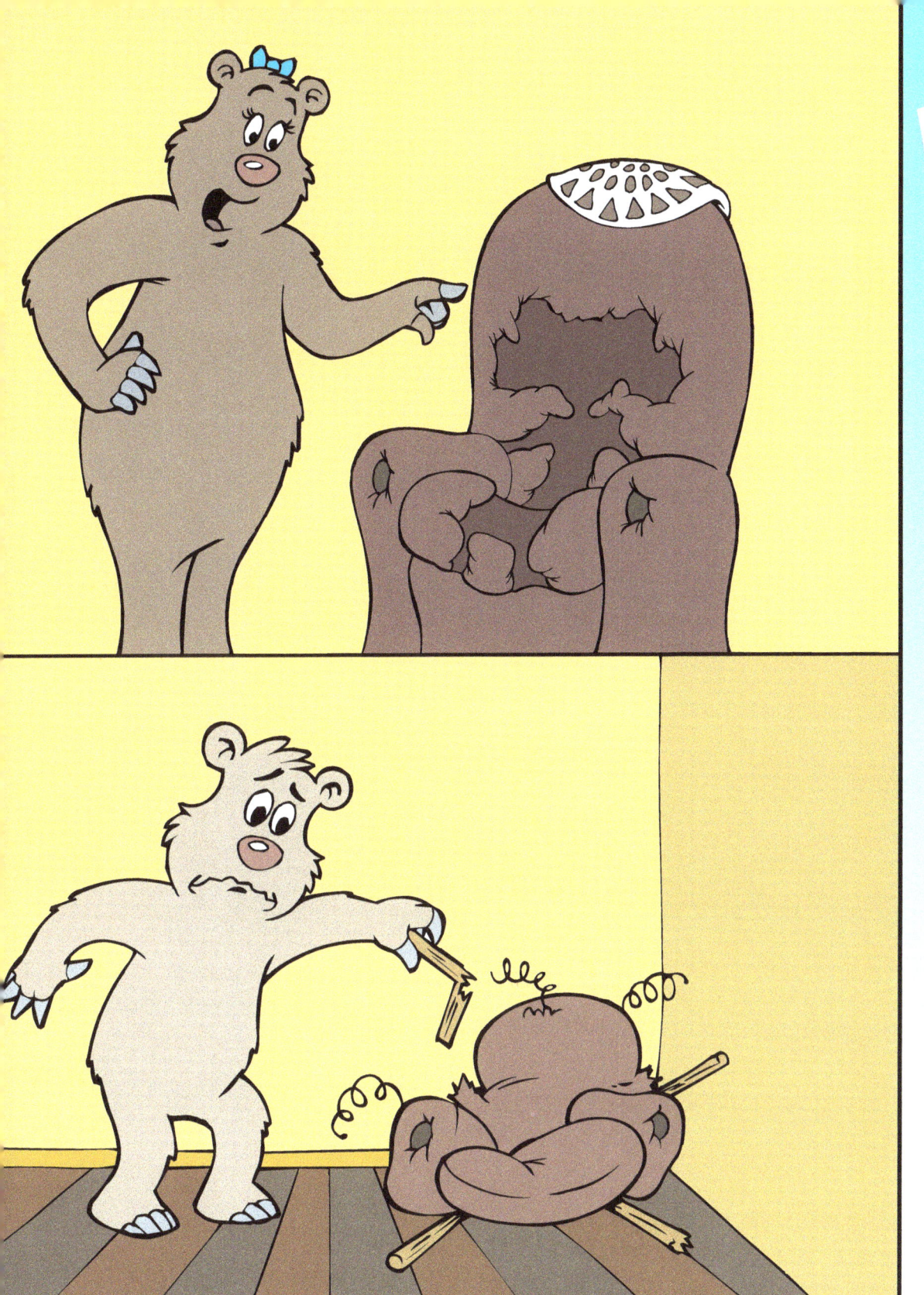

"And someone's been sitting in MY **kursah** and broke it into little pieces!" cried the poor **yeled dov**. After all, it was his favorite **kursah**! Suddenly, the

dov family heard snoring coming from the bedroom, so they went in to look. Something wasn't right. "Someone's been sleeping in my **mitah**!" said the **abba dov**.

"And someone's been sleeping in my **mitah**" said the surprised **ima**. "And someone's been sleeping in MY **mitah** and there she is!" shouted the **yeled dov**.

Just then, Goldilocks woke up and saw the entire **dov** family! Well, the **dov** family thought the little **yaldah** was very **ra'ah** to use their **bayit**

without permission! So, Goldilocks said to the **abba dov**, "Oh, *todah* for letting me eat food from your **ke'arah**, sit in your **kursah**, and lie in your **mitah**!" Goldilocks

said "*Todah!*" again expecting the **dov** family to say, "*Al lo davar!*" But they were angry that she caused so much trouble in their **bayit** and the **dov** family growled

at her. So, she slowly stood up on the **mitah** of the **yeled dov**, and nervously said, "Well, *todah* for having me and... *Le'hitra'ot!*" And with that, Goldilocks jumped off the **mitah**, and dashed out the front **delet**, running as fast as each *kaf regel* could move. Needless to say, she never, ever returned to the *bayit* of the **dov** family again!

Level 3 contains words from Levels 1 & 2, plus all NEW words!

For more HEY WORDY! products, visit...

www.ingramcontent.com/pod-product-compliance
Lightning Source LLC
Chambersburg PA
CBHW042031100526
44587CB00029B/4376